Ground-truth

poems by

Molly Damm

Finishing Line Press
Georgetown, Kentucky

Ground-truth

ACKNOWLEDGMENTS

Thank you to the editors of these journals, in which the following poems first appeared:

Sugar House Review: "Friendship"
Western Humanities Review: "Working Alone," "Walking Home: Map and
Compass"
Sou'wester: "Again and Again," "Cartogram: Defining a Bird"
Terrain.org: "At Sleeping Bear," "Postcard from a Beginner," "Letter to Hugo from
      the Clark Fork"
Drunken Boat: "Vacilando Territory Blues"
The Colorado Review: "If you are a hunter of fossils"
The Collagist: "For When your Male Friends are Asleep"
Copper Nickel: "Poem for the Langley-Porter Hospital"
The Owl Eye Review: "Ellipses," "Dream Dictionary"
Cavalier Literary Couture: "Out of the Blue, and into the Black"

Thank you: Squaw Valley Community of Writers for providing the early space for some
of these poems to take shape. I will always be grateful to the University of Virginia for the
time and support they provided me to write. I would particularly like to thank the staff and
faculty at UVa, namely Lisa Russ Spaar, Rita Dove, Paul Guest, and Gregory Orr, as well as
Jocelyn Sears, Chelsey Weber-Smith, Celeste Lipkes, and Greg Solano for your keen eyes
and care with my work during our time together. To the Charlottesville family, particularly
Kayti Wingfield Sewell and Jennifer Marley Owen, for all of the continued love, support, and
fun. To Jeff de Bellis for a friendship that has meant the world. Montana family, including
earth, sky, water, mountains: gratitude. And most of all, my parents and brother, deep love.

Publisher: Leah Maines
Editor: Christen Kincaid
Cover Art: Billy Renkl
Author Photo: Jen O'Brien Cheek
Cover Design: Elizabeth Maines McCleavy

Printed in the USA on acid-free paper.
Order online: www.finishinglinepress.com
            also available on amazon.com

Author inquiries and mail orders:
Finishing Line Press
P. O. Box 1626
Georgetown, Kentucky 40324
U. S. A.

Table of Contents

For my family

Cartogram: Defining a Bird

When we want everything to change
   we call on the map. We think we find
      the right word for it: *azimuth,*

hour angle, this is how we go on.
   When we want to lose ourselves,
      our marks are light as one

stitch, slow-going: how a canyon opens.
   Remember navigating even the underside
      of the map, its folds so worn. Hardly standing

in a dimness in which memory
   is also the expansion of light.
      Remember setting it down so

gently upon our palms as if by the touch
   we knew each potential dwelling and how
      it rooted. We could stay

where we are. We could daub a home of any
   shape. Suddenly, there's a slender circling
      kestrel, its high *killy-killy* bell-ring

hovering. Suddenly, within its passage,
   bore-full into the April wind, we rise against
      the loneliness of being tethered

here, dwelling only for each
   other, rushing forward just to put it all
      back so deep and quick

into the earth. There's that moment
   of getting brighter. Then there's right before
      you swallow the ghost.

I

*I still have within me the lust to search for living water
with quiet talk to the rock or with frenzied blows.*

Yehuda Amichai

Signal Fire

Say you've reached a moment where: so this is how I learned
                                                            to love—
          And it makes a form, hot bowl of water in the mouth.

Blank milk morning, a bow but not touching, the scattered chance
          of devotion—

You knew and made the signal for yes.
                                        Lightly, lightly: my/your body,
drafts and drafts of us on the corner
                              of endless and
                                        It's called belonging to:
               a speaking low
into your ear in the bath, or spooking up
from a black
               dream or sometimes wanting to be paid for it—

It's not with my eyes I know how:
                    open beacon/full our music island/the hallowed yowl
                              and beg of longing, the way it knows
                                        us, even as devotion

cleaves away.

Say you're in a moment where you
          want to be more moored, less spark, less full, more

          reedy nests between my/your body, faithful to nothing

                    but our aquiline feathers, our own blood harbor.

Blind Date with Freddy, 1963

I have been thinking of the daughter
I would like to have.
From here, should I mark her more
as shining, or rust?

I haven't agreed to never see you again,
just because we're lost in those two
or three other pleasures skimmed open
for us. If her map had a legend,
would it be the traveler
would it be the bear, trundling away.
If the map were to bring you anything
what would it be?
Alive as fire.

I'd never wish unrivaled beauty
for her. If she had a map
it wouldn't bring her love, even riverine,
or sight. What the blue swath offered
the green of holy and swallowing,
bright being, long aubade.
At first glance you may pray
more evening, I too think
this is magical terrain.

Because we must forget
the ease of touching, we are forbidden
to count the seasons since we touched.
How to feed the way I am thinking
of you now, and whether there are
limits to being afraid
to be alive that way.

Marry me before there is any more
science to refute it.

Ellipses

When I snuck into the garden to press
rosemary across your cheeks,
I believed it was to keep nothing
with me. As the distance from Pacific
to day moon shimmered in the heat,
I promised to keep myself empty
for the common names of things.
Say it this way, say it that way,
say nothing. Today I want pure electric
amnesty, save the slack: Tack me down hard
into any scene where moonlight carves
parabolas onto the skin.
Lover, if someone
is hiding you, you can come
out now. If we are two
bodies, I want them to at least originate
from a creek, or some other fluent
topography. I loved the transparencies
in school where we examined sets and subsets,
diagrams, and then later, the body,
but they forgot to expand on the heart:
the depth of its cavities, how it comes unglued
during certain tides. If I made a Venn-
diagram now, I would shape it
like your hips and when I held it up
to the light I would follow the ellipses—
say, follow, say, farther,
I would fall recklessly
into your mouth.

Poem for the Langley-Porter Hospital

(Please keep all windows closed to prevent birds from entering)

As it turns out, you can't have me.
I live my life in widening circles, and in these circles
only birds are entering. Once a blue heron for a week
of mornings the Colorado river split open
like a diamond, and once three condors swirling low
across the Andes, late on an afternoon, chips of obsidian
riding the solstice light. Barred owl, nightjar,
jackdaw, thrush: I give them a home
inside my body. I prevent almost nothing
from entering. Not a goshawk, not the screamers,
not the smoke of your eyes—

Go to Freud, then Jung, then read a textbook,
then read a fairy tale, is one girl's counsel
for a crisis. Some advice is priceless,
but when we talk about our problems, another guy thinks out loud:
Al Queda? 2012?
And the doctors say, Could you be more specific, like, something
more related to yourself? And in this circle
nothing is hidden, not dark cuts nor our desire
to never love anything, ever, ever again or to hop on
unmarked busses or what do you mean by Radical Acceptance?
By Interpersonal Effectiveness?

I read somewhere that in 1972 the Brooklyn Tabernacle's
spark was almost out, but then the holy spirit
lit a fire that couldn't be quenched. Is that what
this is, just fire's refusal to be extinguished?
The lover imitating a diver, then a squirrel in autumn,
the choir initiating a love for everything
in the person who stops on the corner to listen.
The shoe-shine boy barely feeding
his brother with the tiny coins I give him.
The fog has hovered somewhere else
for weeks now, stringing a brightness

through everyone's eyes. I speak too loudly, and too often,
I will prove I am still alive,

and I will not take up with the quiet here,
not for screams we don't hear or the soft wing-beats
of the birds you can't prevent from entering.

Dear One Triptych

Precipice, marrow, parts we
borrow, blood repeating

across our spines. The night you leave
skin warps under another.

Blondest fox darts, brief paste upon the rutted road
deer darts next. All I see are the low things:

delicate imprint of hoof and paw, endless mountain
mud we crossed, re-crossed

swearing low into the brush.

*

If what goes on the canvas
goes first inside us, the briefest moment

and yet there's the imprint: hoof and paw.

If this tailspin into music,
cello waiting to be glued and strung

the skin over our eyes
flooding back at each memory.

*

To be taught quiet, then forget
but silence more a reckoning

memory more brick than companion.
I understand this is one limit of the story:

we are too small a space for what we long
to spin into, press up against.

Our work was just beginning
to save us. Now it's just a sip

of moon turning and then
turning away.

Postcard from a Beginner

Sometimes the hush was so devout we were afraid to move.
—Adam Zagajewski

If it hadn't been for the way your hands ran
over me so supine in the field-
grass if the timothy and sedge and music
the cicadas the forage
if not for the offering
we made knowing someday
the meadow would swamp
the lucky stars would shake us open
like going knee-deep in the river
cold and familiar the way we try to
keep burning once submerged—
      Once you let a suggestion
feel better than any golden turn
every single morning I know you
even though the canopy aches
and through it we see nothing
I know there's a version in which
I am as stunned by the disappearing
movement of dusk
across the pasture as I am by the
hush of how our bodies
can begin in a room and end
in the ground by also the sounds
we make amidst what light outstrips
the pain of knowing if I did not forget
this along with your body so full
of summer
each day as it reels to a close I would surely
stop breathing

Working Alone

Celeste writes about ne-pen-thes and I misread *"A drug mentioned by Homer
that lets one forget sorrow,"* which startles but I always think: *snow.*
One winter in the Blue Ridge, my torso laced
between a farmer's thighs, warm twisting sheets
by the morning flooded
with cold, the stove long-dead.
To be hewn from a thing as vulnerable
as his animals then, huddling, coats dry and sparked
with frost. I wanted to be him, working alone. I wanted
to declare it a bad year
as I sat up in his bed and measured
that it did not belong to me,
everything I observed.
I came to the mountains
to be re-introduced to the other
deaths, the variations: early indigo
morning, its faith
in lingering darkness,
what came according to the coldest
dream in which one can live.
Darkness? Just the need
to hide our own.

Walking Home: Map and Compass

I keep coming back to this bond
with the declination of the body.

It changes as I walk:
difference between true and magnetic.

Difference between a cavity
and the blast of dust which fills it.

What startles most in you is the roaring in of deep weather. The way
I am balmed by it: bent day, captive day, bright cusp.

From out here, I can't hear your wife murmuring her scripture,
or wince as she gently clinks her ring against the table.

All I see are knots, favorites as ones that attach separate cords together,
tresse or call it: *zeppelin bend*. Talisman of your birth,

blood going bitumen despite us.
I think of everything but you as cheap-fired

and roughshod. Whatever can be riven, riven.
Your clear voice husbanding her

from the cease and burn.
It's nothing you can promise between bullet and pill.

Except when I learn you are gone
you're already curled and

ended inside me and I made my own way like that
but never supported it.

Maybe I love you more for coming up
so much as ricochet and giving me a thing to hold or

a tiny thing to ask after
in this separation by fire.

After the Sweat

Bend as one would fully
        over their best invention: a fever diving
                        the night into ifs & afters
                stitching prayer

through the Northern Cheyenne's
            lunar umbra   heat stealing equal
                                        parts of us

help me on the night
        of the sweat to stay seated as the river rock
                        cracks
                into two halves in the sparking
        black grass,

                                remember a healing sent out
        before shimmying   into the Montana early winter's
                                grasp flame still live

between the press of oblivion
        and this house of sky
                                        I hope to be let into

                        after a chill has numbed
        the excess someday bend as one would fully
                towards their teacher or a chapel
                                begin again, but I wish you'd know
                        how impermanent

we are like a warm twilight, like a silver pool
            bereft of fish, how deeply
                        we will shake and then

forget each other.

Up Nights

Memorizing the details
of our lives so far
into each other's ears to grieve
him your grandfather a painter and you
a sculptor and me a painter too
we are so alike we are sewing
memory into our skin with yellow
thread so it will be visible
even as night comes

We're up nights with nothing in the belly
but *Dark Side of the Moon*
and I am on the floor of your bedroom
getting so high I can't walk
to church in the morning
and you are unclasping
my cotton bra to slip it
slowly off
you slide it down

I want to be up tracing
the damp path towards
your house from mine

want to run
towards a hidden doorway
which I will enter no matter what
is behind it if you remember to send
at least a postcard from the mountains
or to think of the night
in the mountains where we slept
on the floor and waited for each other
to become

I can no longer afford to not address you
but there have been winters harder

Mornings are clear, then clouded
no coming, going, no looking beyond,
shuddering towards an afterlife

See we're standing in your old
kitchen and someone's whispering
as we rise to listen it's just so clear

and pure it hurts
it's just us, isn't it?

returning

Lines for Alex After the Party

How beautiful and deep down   all of it seldom
touching

or ever reading the body   open   the way one might
the prospect   of a lover   but calling out

if winds could   these would shatter

we tend to return home   to crystalline silence   distance
danger on peaks   climbing and descending our lonely

symmetry   you know the hard sounds   don't bite

but you like a blast   something inside
no longer shutting fully   after

so that every place I go   your voice inside
arcs and then   holds   there's a borderline

as if we could point   there's what hurts
but would never tell it

*

Light a candle   for pure attention or
how to make a thing   unwhisker from frost

a lot of you in the grass   I never thought of
a lot fed back through   each morning

like a flume   think of the Valle Sagrado   the oracle
I would take you to   spicy like dancing   after

the party   the weird medicine of it
the slow-twitch kiss   in tethered dark

I love you strangely   you bird in the mouth

For When Your Male Friends Are Asleep

Maybe some darks are deep enough to swallow what we want them to.
—Mary Szybist

Maybe we fling our hair
to be demure but on the way stars
on our necks. Maybe they prick.
Maybe we swallow like a river,
maybe in the dark we're porous
as the wet in it. Concussed
by the bedding of stones there,
could be we're blurred but
at our best like that.

Whatever violence in being snowblind,
better than the butter leather
burn of slow glances and bump
in the house. We'll never be
as forbidding but we wanted to be
a softer landing than that, more contact,
more breath left for crossing the bridge,
or for a best friend at my cellar door
in the cool, mineral afternoon.

I've taken only a thimbleful of love
out of love
for you and our scary
appetites. Someday we'll lose this
what each other sounds like
lose the field to brush
and trouble, we'll pray:
maybe some darks will push
back. Pray:
take me while the rhythm's
still good.

Hologram

Most of my regrets come from water: & the stutter of defending
where we are: a collapsing of the clairvoyance that brought you
this strength: equal parts jade stone and the first gold
of high beams on ice: touching the nape of a neck without
citing each moment as kin: enjoying the chat: enjoying the opaque
of certain conditions: the little clearing we leave

for the broken: parting in train stations the technique of position
and image changing big: like if our backs or ankles could
emboss rock: the underlying crescent: or maybe no one
noticed that we walked away: tensile hearts: & the way
we are beginning to cascade: pairs of boats the oil
whirring around them in the harbor: who you are

opened me up: tying the fragile knot.

Friendship

The code word for the night is
blow. As in, *I'll sell you a bag of*
and you might wonder what I'm doing
here listening to compatriots a little less
folksy than I'd like for Montana
with my cheeks aflare it's true
I'm only pointing out
the quick way to flock towards
anonymity especially when it makes
me blush and though I don't mention
my mother to the stranger
from Natchez it would be best
if he knew her his need
to talk is so muscular I'll talk
to anyone whose voice is that
dappled I'll talk to anyone
the night such a torrent
of otherwise, silence.
You likewise
might wonder why she appears
I too wonder it's one of those tricks
dear reader, that I don't know
the trick to, but she's a suite
of strange notes evaporating
into joy & she'll talk to anyone
no matter the weather
so for now, she'll stay. Tonight,
she's asking of her own mother
as cardinal dazed on suet in the suburbs
to play a little less bridge and do a little more
praying that I'll marry someday
and if I had to admit
anything it's that when the bartender
offered cocaine to everyone
to rescue them from something
or this town in the rain
I was thinking about all of the tiny

candles barely snapped to flame
before their shimmery reverie
made waxy the cake I was thinking
about nesting in the packet of her arms
for so many years
while everyone else yelled
blow.

II

If you are a hunter of fossils

Around a bend, and light that erases
such failure. As a kid, in a desert
full of fragile soils and beauty buckled
and spired, full of hoodoo-tent-rock, space
that could have drowned us.
And the lakes cast pink, dowsing
for the ley lines in blueberry
bush and frost dune and there's something
I want to tell you about the intervening
hunt and divine. It wasn't all Peace be with you
and then the wheels fell off,
not all duck duck and then
there's a bang and the goose is another
slow learner, stoic in soft blonde
moccasins. Flannel here, linen there, a little bit of tulle tutu
magic tossed in for the ballerina dream,
which no one originally believes
is a danger. I could crouch and crouch
within the invisible and never, ever
disappear. Which isn't what anyone wanted
but me, pinky swear. But then there's a rush
and no one dreams the seam of a self
could be blown at birth and a child
would emerge and always wonder.
All the long way to saying, it's a secret,
the deluge and the compendium
shaped like a narrative but fighting
with a small child who just wants to know
was I touched? And has all of this long
division into cells and ventricles
and fear of bodies a way of saying:
surprise. Yes. You had a good healer mother who never
unsheathed the right knife on the right
man, or at least never knew to. What
can we trust of our memories?
Never ever that they quietly pull
paint across the shutters and fade

baked in the sun. But that they travel
and gambol like passengers
in a story book, beloved and fantastic,
wrought hot and bent new.

I'm in my girl body now, foraging around
and no one knows the answer
but me, me, call on me, if I ever learn to love.
If I ever figured out a thing about love,
it was from disease mind and the way it enters
the currents of a child through eyes
that she doesn't want looking, hands
that she doesn't want near.
I've run out of ways
to bubble around it. If you are a hunter
of fossils, then I'm in charge
of celebrations, and promise me, promise it,
I'll even peel off my sparkling nets for you,
because if we can't celebrate
everything that came after,
I will fold and undevote
and also with you
it will be the way I die.

Vacilar

So it is good
to rise

for your story

but to remember
that memory
harvests
and locks.

It is best
to be loved
in your story

but save loved
truth is
save refuge
there is
nothing.

The romance of orienteering:

Searching for where the inner fills with stone or light or fiction, absence or
lightning or waiting to move through the dream.

Vacilando: going somewhere but not greatly caring whether or not you get
there, although you have direction.

Parts of a compass: base plate, direction of travel arrow, housing, needle,
cardinal points, degree dial.

I am one hand in each hand
of my father's. I am walking
up his legs until his stomach
where I tilt back and flip
and my body circles
through the summer air.

I am one hand in each hand
of my father's. I am in a basement,
with a mirror, being quiet.
I am trying to draw
my body, what lies
under the skin
of my face. I rub
it out, tear the paper,
start again.

My ears are cupped
in my hands. Voices
rise shrill in such a stunned
sweep I imagine
one has hurled glass
or fire.

I cover the mirror
with my body,
I cover the drawing
with my hands
and my voice
begins to fade.

                    *

I am one hand in each hand
of my father's. I am in a pine,
high above the yard,

and the branches hold
as I disappear.

They have cocktails below,
and for a moment forget

and for that moment I stay
and the lake is there

like a sleeping breath,

and beyond that, the river
brushing Canada,
and somewhere inside,
a cache of maps.

                    *

I am one hand in one hand
of my father's, the other
in my brother's,
they swing my body high
between them as we walk.
Sunday has its own
voice, greedy shelter
against the winter.
I wander the church hallways
because I will not
be made to listen, or pray
slip in for communion
and turn away from the wine
because I am a child
and save the little wafer, the body,
for later in the white yard
where I can sing.

                    *

To learn
without light. For a wind
from each direction
to argue
for its path. The inside
is a peninsula and the landed
end is bedrock. The ocean
end contains geological
time and between them
rifting, amassing.
Write in darkness.
Register nothing,
keep walking.

Midnight Poem with Neighbor, Glimpsed

No one took him as a believer you'd
see him mornings fencing the static or
overturning the mower
look at that they'd say repeating their mothers'
Hosanna in the highest at the window they were busy
forgiving those
who trespassed against them in spare bedrooms
where the motif was all eagle and garland go get 'em
America until you were inside
the red leather Cadillac and then that was a different
time. Because the trace
of a pattern to the days wasn't so
broken and you could press anti-venom into the BB'd
squirrel's little wound you could erupt
all your rations to save him after
your brother walked
away with his gun the balcony sighed
whatever happened,
happened because
Sunday was for all the revelation
the taking flight. Or it is tonight.
It's a thinly veiled game
of spoons we play in the TV light waiting
for the right moment
to reach our hands into the gummy cross-fire.
Bold friend, from earlier
in the neighborhood, there's a burnish to autumn
we learn to live with. I confess to you,
I never learned your name. I saw you
out the window in the street with your saw and thought
if I thought hard enough,
I could invent anyone.
I imagined if we all stopped blessing
through our teeth let go the balloon in which we tried
to contain something of our best path we'd be
left with more than just
our own
scorched kingdoms.

Postcards to Katherine

If the dream takes place in summertime, one dreams of volcanic eruptions.
If the dream takes place in late summer, one dreams of building a house.
—The Foundations of Chinese Medicine

1.
Start in, kid: new vibrato and hum.
The world with its icy
in-roads and persistent
shunting. New notches
in our old columns of lust:
someone called it
local color.

2.
Tell me, friend, why an outcrop
of ash? It isn't such a bad thing
to live in one world forever.

3.
For the first time, in fragments,
hell & pitch-perfect explorations
of grief. Fingers pearl over
a rosary, discover a smashed
conch, then: wet smell of an iris,
its lonely intelligence.
For this we are grateful, the way
each body was breakwater,
jetty.

4.
I'll give you one
of everything tonight,
unless you are starving.
I stacked the chairs
in an easy dimness
broke only one
pitcher and its sibling
saucer, when the heart
is weak, one dreams

of fires.

5.
One dreams of laughing.
The kind of freedom
that's worth cementing.

6.
You reading this, hello,
thank you, I wish I could focus
on your eyes. Leap, in the shape
of praise, but do your grace
in different voices.
Even if you don't, I'll pretend
you did.

7.
Shelter me, sister, lover, rusted
corral, re-emerge from the lee
Sierra, from the wise
and wild surfaces we steeped
up slow. The elastic fences in our
gaze. That was bliss.
You were wearing
your house like a rune.

Tectonic in March

The fences bow today
in a loose spring squall. Hoarfrost
stripping March its first
buds along the split-rail.
At first glance you would think
I was trying to stand straight
against it, but I'm fine
with leaning in, that this life
won't be all shotgun
and wood-stove, trembling
inside an invisible love.

You have to be willing to be so
slender and struck inside.
Who are you crushed
like a garden under winter.
I'll see if I can stay
planted in the quicksilver
gale, sit still long enough
to watch something dapple
in the sun, for the ridges to honey
and smear behind the nightfall.

I think he was pointing at the comet,
but I was looking
at his mouth. At where
the lines filled in like dawn around it.
What do you grasp
for, and who reaches back?
In a funny wind, stepping out

of the river's layers, knowing
it wasn't the pyrotechnics
that ever made you
feel long, spirit, and true.

Brother's Almanac

We lived in a mountain
the color of rum. We lived anywhere
two pieces of bread would buy us, leaven and muscle,
big backyard pheasant strutting
through the snow. Say first why the windward slope
is better, why you would carry me there
with no intentions. Big difference if
an avalanche comes. Why have you come?
I would make, I thought when I was young,
a good brother to her.
I'd make a pearl-string for her
when I thought she was growing
beautiful enough. When she called in
from the bully winter for a fighter, I would protect
her, hum and carry all the way home.
Plumage of rain, all the inky faintness
through the windows, she's crying because
I have taped her wrists and ankles together again
it's a hunt for blackberries or Easter eggs and she can't walk
to come. Remember when at the service with our right hands
each a peace sign and jamming them horizontal
to the knuckle *peace, peace* like St. Augustine's
holy kiss. I would be rough except for once,
when I sang to her in her bed half blind with heavy
liquor about a canary or a cockatiel she'll never
remember this I thought except she does.

Field

Late spring storm and oblivion's punching a hole
                                                                    into the most immediate sky,
                                                                                    into the usual ruckus

   of sleep and longing, the open steps of this necessary harvest, getting you
in bits and piecemeal, all the divine afterthoughts

                                                                that come too late after touching
                                                                                        to speak.

There's vice-versa in each taut-line hitch, each mouth of mine
      in the lantern of yours, I tip my hat
                                                    to begged chances

                                    and the best journeying between river and roost,
sharp-shinned and laughing, clutch/slip, each blessing

about the size of a valley, the weight of a creek sluicing through.

               I look through your letters constantly—the things we thought
                                                    to save
                                        in words, little tintypes and quicksands,
                           our secret words were: wolverine, or better: beginner's noon,

      our words for not there, or not yet, or I'm still vaulting

into the abyss. When the buck fell in my last dream, and you
      dressed it in the blue that means winter is coming, we made of the field

            a carved box and intaglioed ourselves
                                                    inside it, naked as a bone.

Binary

Somewhere in Detroit, my sister
steps onto a balcony. She leans out
into the summer and the pots of Primrose
and Moonflower don't begin
to pulse, exactly, but everything
in the night shifts
towards her. She points the telescope
at Arcturus: it will keep expanding
before shedding its outer
shell, she offers slowly when she finally
speaks. Her voice is an opening
during which the evening
fills, overflows.

Her voice is the field
you are standing in when your eyes begin
to adjust to the tin burn
of one, and then a companion star,
and then their splitting.
Because it is a new small continent
of light, her voice begins
to dismantle me.

If I have been alone my whole life,
if I have been sleeping beside a fire
and the backs of my knees have been dusted,
and my neck has been dusted
with ash if somehow my mother
is a jar I didn't bloom fast enough inside,
then maybe my sister and I
share this.

So I am sketching her there, into the evening,
and as she comes into focus
so does a dwelling inside me
which single stars cannot attain alone.
This sister she will live and die

as a white dwarf star,
planetary nebula blackest
she nameless, she bright.

Jazz at Young Writers

It's a little bit about death, she says, it has to do
with falling away. The music is what is inside
the music, is what you cut away.
See, every time you hear it, it will be different,
you'll be the environment more and more.
Same Bach, same *Love Supreme*, skirts tucked
even higher in the fear of being gone.

He played a double bass ocarina to her little bit
of death, and I thought about Anne Spencer's
garden today, all the words dissolving inside it
all the forever and opportunities we know
are wrong but do anyway
you forbidden minuet
I would miss so much sleep if it meant
never having to be alone.

Line of Sight

After Henri Cartier-Bresson

In my sky-stricken mind, I point
a meadow towards you.
It's the way it is neither sudden
or curtaining the future
that I love.
Spindrift sifts the length,
sap not yet frozen
in its line. Who knows what luminous
things we conceal
from each other.

I believe in one whose palms
lift the cloud
up over the mountain. If you can't feel life
in that, our father
will say. He is
calling to young women in the streets
as the protests die around him.
Our father becoming dizzy
as he begins to carry the snow.

And my sister closes her eyes
but just for a moment.
Because it is April now,
her pink coat is mostly unbuttoned
her thin legs new and bare as a colts'.
She is pretending
to be blind, one being
with the air in the alley.

Our father is a giver of birdseed
and refuge. Alone in his room,
his three favorites perch atop
a domed cage. Their white bodies
almost pierce

the shadows, but instead turn dove grey
and fade. He holds one in his fist

to imprint its tiny musculature there
before going to paint. Our father is devoted
to nothing besides these birds,
turpentine
and unkempt night.

Our mother died this morning,
but for years she lay topless, prone
as a fallen sculpture each morning
after another man left.
We covered her
and propped her in the sun
while the neighbors hummed
their low songs, wet laundry glittering
in their hands,
turning a half-blind eye.

The best lovers are out
pacing the hallways. Not a string of desires,
an opening in sight. Tell me into the broad
of my back where my yellow dress breaks
and beads off into skin. Tell me I will walk
again. Say this is what it sounds like,
little girl with fallen letters and wanting out,
to survive.

Signal Fire II

Say you're in a moment where—so this is how I learned to speak—
Say you've gambled and won, culled a teaspoon of the bright and grand,
lengthened imperceptibly in your body towards this voice.
Suddenly there is a chance we will reach each other
through all of this wild dim, though I'm asking to quietly tear it
open and to darken a surface for our zenith, our nadir,
whatever comes in and comes through.

It's true I lied about the horses,
about that first dream. Where I lay down with them in their warmed hay
because I like the pokey grace they stand around in
until you spur them to dance
and then they dance. But it was so dangerous: smashed thin-as-a-flag body,
stitched-into-strips body, ferry-me-across-the-water body,
mine when it finally rose ethereal,
rose crushed. So this is how I learned to—

and dance, Boatman, *flood*. Each Christmas when I stole the baby
Jesus from where he slept
in the crèche, supine furl of his tiny
porcelain limbs in their swaddling clothes,
each night just tried to keep him safe
beside me.

Now III

Two is two; February the only month we loved.
Like a story requested so many times
         it turns incandescent
remember that this could happen anywhere.

Blue departure, I'm jittery as a child's flute,
         Stille Nacht, Heilige Nacht—
The still-light touch of
                  only the close, most holy couple
My arms are so heavy.
Father, why is there always someone
leaning against me?
         o wie lacht Lieb'—
How will it end?
So far no luck in rendering the goddesses obsolete.
                  oh how laughs
                  love out of your divine mouth.
I am all dressed for each gorgeous continent.

Useless here: the best
of the best of imagination. You have to go into an absence
you may never return from, the body
         Schlaf in himmlischer Ruh!—
as a February sea, spring a glint in a soft
throat—what shivers
around a string of trespasses

mostly incognito, yet. I was this single crocus

peeking, Father. Sleep in heavenly
love
out of your heavenly mouth—

You secret, incarnate thing
the war's still on.

Dream Dictionary

I wanted to know about humus like I wanted to know about ricochet
chalice chimera big loose country bones like I wanted to know
about work. Ricochet was a brother gone, the sharp aluminum
crack-back of that. Look up, pea. He was one of those people
for whom talking and emotion were the only parts:
light on light.

A chalice the moon grew long from, poured the lake into,
dissolved as our body. Bones were what streaked underneath. When I say
the sun exploded it is not hyperbole, neither am I trying to spell the edge
of a story. I mean the mountains below it suddenly poured
headlong over the skin of our hands. We don't always love that burning
yet we are here. And where the sun was slightly thrummed.
The most unabashed thing is light on light on light. The fact-checker
still talks like that, even as he clears away the places where dead stars
have intertwined.

To make amends I rubbed soil into the lowland of his back, he said he dreamt
a heron perched there. Summer is an adze
that peels the bark from our skin, and the place
where lightning rings out, totems
of smoke. Let us awaken,
let us pivot once
and take flight.

Unshelter

Ourselves akimbo, the escarpment slammed with rain.
Teton, Talkeetna, I'm working only to tell the story
I never heard.

Pine-knot, slip-knot, everything concentric and gathering
like lightning, suddenly we're shedding our layers in the obvious
pierce of morning, and I'm being named

out loud like a bale in a meadow, which is to say
not at all. Sentinel of spruce were you sister or brother
and can one hand keep the rhythm

while the other slowly dives. At the core is a fin
and in some places the slick fish answers if you let down
your hands and what anchors

and what travels. Through the weak-tea morning, who is it
that arrives to score into your center
their pulse, a flash that never leaves you.

III

The road is fresh and aches...

Tomaž Šalamun

Letter from Arbutus

At some point, you'll return
to each place that destroyed you. Mercy will grab
your wrist on the long dock when you think

you are already gone.
Be the birch bark canoe it arrives in.
Be the way it slices the lake clean

like a penknife through an envelope,
like the August horses' flanks
as they slid between our thighs.

The summer of cantering through
the lupine on twig
legs, bending down just once

to taste the salt lick so unfamiliar
to city kids once to make sure
it was what it seemed, of spoken code all the way

to the barn barely able to steer
our bodies the way we would later struggle
with the Appaloosas and Geldings

galloping hard into the river
and even later the sticky clutch
and shudder of our mother's car

as we left the polo field silent
clicking the seats upright,
just learning about regret.

Mercy, we scream-sang as we jerked each other's
fingers backwards to flat, my friends and I,
mercy mercy mercy.

After lights out, thick as spies wasted
on bourbon milk we outlined Annie Oakley
in our dreams. We traced our names done in glow-

in-the-dark paint above our beds, *to have*
telling a silent story to *to want*. When we awoke
lake in our hair, and the rifle's

kickback still bruised our palms.

Back home, the game was drawing
tiny bodies we wanted to impose
over our tiny own and trim away

the excess, fat or bone, we stenciled them out and
who'd go back there? He brought her
coffee then, watched the milk

bloom up through. I'm still unsure
if at that point we were the singer, or what's barely
remembered of the song.

Letter to Hugo from the Clark Fork

There's a delicacy and strength to it, quietly waiting within how many first
frosts for the next line to come. Quietly waiting, the lace of the night lake
rising there's a reverence soothing over the rocks there's a delicacy in the shine
to it. Some part of us knows a home upon entering and remembers when
it enters us, also how. Wishing to know you, I go and kneel by the water. I take off
what glows on me I let fall what begs to. In these granite cathedrals, some part of us
remembers the wind whipping through. You were right to ask the current:
make me better. I ask a hundred things
of the river. Copper water from Butte feathering
over the backs of rocks, I let fall in the gin jar from my hands.
I want something to be crushed or carried away
and want it not to be me tonight. I beg the courage it took to stand up
and scatter backwards the man stepping straight into the fire
while everyone else ate and laughed. I ask you protect him, delicate man,
strong man, let no one burn tonight. Let the horses stamp
dust gently in the dark. Sometimes, *what thou lovest best*
remains a ghost. The silence we carry's just
as good a home as any we could make. Up late, this valley fills
with music. It's our kind of loose strength. It's our way of stepping forward,
whispering out and swimming on.

Porch Song in April

This is a forgotten passage
I enter and exit outside of time
I see the fig there
and in the first moment
since last summer I can eat

it is blooming a hard unripe
turned gorgeous supple splitting
and the whipping in of summer
unfurling leaves and the air
I cup my hands to hold it

sudden thigh-high thistles up
and with them no-name weeds up
would-be yard overnight
I am no longer shuttered in here
I am tall stepping out

and shaking meanwhile I lean
into the shadow as it descends
like an intricate breathing
in the upper rooms I am
a certain spacious knockoff

of myself I flicker against
stillness and measure hours
and in those hours come
un-nested
torch my aerie

I pirouette and
imagine nothing
more fragile than
the need
to take flight

Ground-truth

They took a drive one autumn
pieced Iowa to Nebraska and parted

after resting for an hour at dawn against
the Colorado line. No mountains

in sight. They took a drive, they were following closely
to one another and she wanted to ask: which are you

brother or lover, because if you are going to be my shadow

I will set you on fire. Or I will husk you
from your clothes and spare you, because news

travels fast. But she couldn't ask. The last time
they were together in the mountains, he skied off the roof

the Highwaymen came on they went and had New Years,
champagne in the whiskey and skin showing.

The lake could've ignited with desire.
Then he married young and quietly, became a soldier.

She thought being a man must be gunning the sky

must be never seeing the land under
the dead you make. Wanted to show him the wolves

and birds he made of scrap metal when his hands
were all love and dirt. There is no uniform

for sculptor. You think it always circles back but
dear oblivion, dear sky, you madman,

it doesn't always circle back.

Now I watch her try to do with men
what she wanted only his body

to cover. There was an emptiness
they tempered in each other.

Lover, brother, you shuttered animal: maybe as neither will he come.
No mouth on the shoulder, Christmas blessings,

to have said *I give up* she will not do;
but what is he, his eyes or fingers gone.

Out of the Blue and Into the Black

After Edith Södergran

I am nothing, plus the idea of young rust,
which insists upon metal to darken.
I am pointing at Saturn to learn my cardinal directions.
I am a Zyprexa elixer, Abilify amplified, Seroquel's seductress,
Geodon's bright home. I am milligrams and milligrams
of shy side effects. I am partially checking in here
based upon my hidden knowledge of wire.

I am the feeling of oh god, but soaked in rain.
I am building something into the outback
of the mind. Here I am: still keeping my skirts down
even throughout the full Niagra
of night. I am splitting the distance between bruised hips
and eating dirt, and I'm having a second life cycle
with the days I thought I lost.
I am the man slung like a dead deer
across the morning doorstep and I am the cherries
I give him. Tonight I am folded,
like water, back into the skirts of the hills.
I am ramming my silky body
into the spaces between stones.

I am the soft diagnosis:
You need mindfulness, I am the river's rap-
white soothe. I'm each friend who wonders
what are you doing there I am learning,
from the prolific fish runs, how to preserve food
year round. I am learning to stay drunk
on nothing so reality cannot destroy me.
I am standing on the peak of Divisadero
where you can see everything, plus the idea
of mountains, whose plates are always
broken, who rise there and insist—

Tremolo

Had to come in out of the weather.
Nothing, plus a downpour, read:

Broken waking, punctuated by the honeyed tail
of an old dream. He's always hulking

when we reconsider the evening, I'm standing
in a frosted Easter and in the morning

sunlight calms the muddy snow. The street empties
into the shoreline as if to explain

all of this hum and watching
and our feel of taut taut between the spheres.

It would be easier to explain reading patterns
in the ash, but in with this sweep of damp, nothing left—

I felt like once I caressed the empty, I could go.

I learned by holding to the thicket of a stranger
that sometimes the body has wires

crossed so deep no fingers dare untangle,
felt like the mind's sickness was a river

I belonged to. I had come in
from the far edge of the mountain for an exquisite

invitation: I mouthed no.
For the first time in a dry county

I did not stumble, knuckle up,
I did not beg a drink.

Last News from the Lower Elevations

The hardest part of touching is that everyone
says yes, the sun and wind agree to yes,
it's a miracle that yes is here and here, no, sorry,
I meant here here
here but then at some point it means I will
carry you all of you or it means start backing away.

Today I was feeling brave, so I said
the flesh, you can have it, the voice,
let us not forget it rises, the heart,
my coalfield, let you carry me somewhere
that hasn't answered yet.

What I Remember, May

When I think of your brother who lived
with quiet sickness and never knew it,
pressing into each new town
in a startlingly fresh suit,
when I think of him staring
at a lit patch of concrete from his hallway
window the mind half opaque
half your average full-body nightmare.
It's always the wrong kind of erasure
imagined landscape of true darkness
save the gibbous light save the waning,
except there's no always but for this.
When I think of how sick
I was in San Francisco that year, the absolute secret
of it, the nurse who came to stay and tenderly
dose the breaking. When I imagine
his own doctor mishandled him the way one might
absently drop a china cup, and how
he was nearly your twin
in photographs, when I imagine the contrasts
between one May and the next,
I know there will never be
another likeness, a precision of bloodlines
like that. My friend, we're standing
together and doing nothing
but landing our breaths
inside this warm evening.
I almost trust you know how to companion
the best of him now.
It's what you see with,
canting towards home.

Poem for Chaupi Road

At three o'clock when I need to pray,
I think of the house in Punta Sal, the stooped men
calling *Where are you going*, their shoulders
heavy with bananas still clasped
at the necks. As the road falls to cliff all around us,
the soda bottle shrines are abruptly abandoned
the road either mud or hard. *What is it*
you were looking for, and always, *vaya*
con Dios. Each chapel of the coast
with its proper saint, the bells in repair
wrapped like bandaged fists, some still ringing
a muffled noon. The Catholic murmurs begin
just as each day, in a breath
of sweet chatter, disappears. The smashed melons in the dirt
are like beautiful, ruined mouths, shimmering
alongside endless shards
of broken glass.

When I need to walk forward, I think
of a thin plywood raft full of fish,
the boy that push-pulls them home
with a long, flat, wooden spoon and the way
the ocean breaks gently around him.
From the road, a line of hovering gulls
is our ongoing correspondence—
Just now one dove so sudden, and alone.

Again and Again

For Horseshoe Canyon

If there is a world, let us be in it.
Let this desert teach us
something about simple
arrivals, and the uncommon passion
of falling through the hours
here, what it's like to search
for water together.
Where there is space
for confluences, take them.
Where there is time
to go deeper, go
until something begins
to ache. Trill, bedrock,
frost on the vetch,
it's a leaning into silence
we sometimes know,
it's as brave as any dangling talk
we could make. Let's build
something new from the
remnants of what is sloughed
by sand and wind
and water and then
I'll say it plain
as I can. Let us be pure
in our allegiance
to one another, and the origins
that keep opening us up.
Shimmy through the slot
and shadow and when
we stretch free, in the damp
end-cove, when we stretch up
into the sun, we will say thank you
for the singing, the raw
the bursting, warm
darkness, clean joy, one pot,
its fullness, the pulling away of stars
before we awaken, the splitting

of their tracks as we sleep. The dust
and the radiance.

Eyrie

To the east, the slow accretion of clouds.
To the west, towards the mountains, copper night.

I forget that in the center
are rivers
unspoken for,

that there are valleys
the strata of which we lower
into, perhaps, in the hollow
between breaths.

In the tiny pause
between the taproot
of summer
and its departure,

I nearly forget the long sieve
of winter, the absence,
the fractional glimpses

of light. Dear one, I will go
without speaking.

Ablaze, keep me
until I disappear.

Au Clair de la Lune

This is how to learn to love:
jump,

but most of my decisions
have been wrong.

Forgive me my absence,
forgive these nights shot through

with velvet,
but on a friendship

level the reason we came
here was to edit out

the after-dark. Tell me your
name, your face, I like the way

they sound, tell me the cleft
glaze of your eyes is impermanent.

Fragile filter, I just wanted
to hear you say it again.

Growing into all of the voices
that barrel-roll through

the mind, magnets and circuits,
by what omen will we know

to lie down in the streets,
to emerge as the carving

between fears and if I'm in charge
of celebrations I'll hold the gate

open for this willingness to be wrong.
Where does your mind go

after years ago thank you
for a predilection towards

survival thank you for closing
a door behind me I found

I could see better then to navigate
the compound,

gathering dark.

Begin Again

But it is good
to step out
of your story.

It is best
to give away
your story

to pay out the coils
of each memory

and begin again,
but please do forward:

* charts from the Langley-Porter Hospital (quiet, mild, asleep, gets
  along well with others)
* ground-truth (ain't too late for anything with a body)

begin again:
but please forward this:

he venido yo coriendo olividando me de ti

He typed his constellations on the inside of her ear

da me un beso pajarito no te asustes colibri

She collected the best places to lie down

he venido encencida el desierto para quemar

Hummingbird cupola in an opening of oaks

porque la alma prende fuego cuando deja de amar

Because the soul sets fire when you stop loving

Oronym

When asked to choose between a world
I love and language that makes me

shake, I choose the cartographer
each time. And each time

let's say I was thinking about
what music it doesn't make, this world,

and what music it does. And the storm
of it is that without fiercely studying

what makes us go up and down about things
it can seem all wrong or just a bright

husk. But what about if we carried everywhere
only the memory of trespassing

the fog between us on that mountain,
the night we invited ourselves in. And what if

when we got there, it was only how desiccated
in the coming and going the air became. Friend,

if ever life were exquisite,
it was how you swept rain from our bed

before dusk that made it so. Now I hear
our song-lines, and they do not die

and reappear incrementally, there's a buzz
to it, a habit or a litany: how soft the inclines

of you, the night that includes you,
our voices made of steel and butter

entirely. Along the road there's pleasure,
clean and angelic, there's char and there's

presence and when night broke so cold
upon us without naming it I should have

never walked away.

Vacilando Territory Blues

i.

It's true to stop listening to the voices
that tumble through the river. To stop waiting for a ballast,
waiting for the level, stop going out at night for walks
and trying to get spiritual, stop thinking about sources
the gates we carry each other through about snow on the ridges,
where it runs to, and all of that silence. I'd rather be lying in the lap of a Porteño
on a bench in a park passing warm orange soda from hot mouth
to hot mouth. Rather than already knowing rather be learning
over and over how to say *let's go* and *you are my brother* words
for *wheelbarrow* for *mud, straw* and *when* and *how about now?*
Let me be ecstatic naked and high in the pines in a darkness
that admits only terrific upwellings of heat deep passage
pray I'll be gilded palm to palm. Rather let the horse
spook and run off into the desert with my bedroll than waltz slowly
around the padded rooms of my heart with my hands outstretched
for the light switch. Again I hear the voice of the friend,
wicked and warbling me to turn on each of the tiny bones
of my ears, to turn on a bold kindness, to cling to the parting smoke
of these full, heavy dreams. And I'd rather have you in a crumbling house than
continue to revise your ghost into a poem, much rather see than all of the looking
hear than all of the listening today I'll burn and in the burning singe, maybe never
even shine upset the balance affix my hips to your hips and make of the heat and
pressure a stone bowl to place at the edge of the sea.

ii.

And whenever I hear Richard Thompson do *1952 Vincent Black Lightning*
just like the other night want to be more like the words I couldn't make out
or misheard want the bar to be darker the touching more sudden
so that I barely have time to kiss your arm around my collarbone
because they say everything that rises
must converge and it's true
I am mixing metaphors and conflating the bodies of most
of the people I love, but if I stay here, and you weld scraps of iron

into a rough box then I will feed it and feed you all day
I will leave everything
to the mystery
you won't believe how clearly, if you'll let me, I'll arrive.

At Sleeping Bear

It's easy enough to say *speak,*
your fingers untangling the hair
of a young girl whose father
is dying. For most of my life,
mortality was a susurrus, breeze
in the white-bark, subtlest thing
on the landscape, easy to miss.
Now I think it has a shape carved
into your palms, one you don't choose
the weight of although it's tender,
gentle as a hymn.

Before me a slope of soft dune
over the lake we climb up from.
It's soft the way trillions of tiny
weathered things make a gentleness
when they pile and there's wind.
Only up there I'd borrow Merwin
to ask *how can we ever be sure*
and my father would say
be always beginning and once
you've begun be all the way
shared the way a lover of birds
can so deeply agree with a lover
of plants on loving the way someone
who is dying agrees
to re-unite,
to exile nothing.

Molly Damm earned her MFA from the University of Virginia in 2014, where she was a Henry Hoyns Fellow in poetry. Her writing has appeared in the *Colorado Review, Drunken Boat, The Collagist, Sou'wester,* and *Western Humanities Review,* among others. In 2018, Molly received an MS in Marriage and Family Counseling from Montana State University, and works as a therapist and Writing Lecturer. Born in Detroit, she lives in Bozeman, Montana.

www.ingramcontent.com/pod-product-compliance
Lightning Source LLC
Chambersburg PA
CBHW021157090426
42740CB00008B/1133